RUSSIAN REPUBLICS

SIMON ADAMS

FRANKLIN WATTS
LONDON•SYDNEY

Designer Steve Prosser
Text Editor Belinda Hollyer
Art Director Jonathan Hair
Editor-in-Chief John C. Miles
Picture Research Diana Morris
Map artwork Ian Thompson

© 2004 Franklin Watts

First published in 2004
by Franklin Watts
96 Leonard Street
London
EC2A 4XD

Franklin Watts Australia
45-51 Huntley Street
Alexandria
NSW 2015

ISBN 0 7496 5542 9

A CIP catalogue record for this book is
available from the British Library.

Printed in Malaysia

Picture credits
AP/Topham: 11, 30, 34
Steve Dupont/Rex Features: back cover, 31
East News/Sipa Press/Rex Features: 28
Earl & Nazima Kowall/Corbis: 32
Novosti (London): 10, 20, 25, 33, 35, 36
Novosti/Topham: 21
PA/Topham: 26
Picturepoint/Topham: 18
Josef Polleross/Image Works/Topham: 38
Popperfoto: front cover b, 12, 14, 15, 17, 19, 22
Jana Schneider/Rex Features: 23
Daniel Sheenhan/Image Works/Topham: 13, 40
Sipa Press/Rex Features: front cover t, 24, 41
Topham: 16
UPPA/Topham: 27
V. Viatkin/Novosti (London): 37

CONTENTS

I TRODUCTIO

In 1991 eight new countries emerged as independent states. Their birth was difficult, and in their short lives they have experienced war, invasion, political instability and dictatorship. Together they form one of the most dangerous flashpoints in the world today.

NEW AND OLD STATES

All eight new states were once part of the Union of Soviet Socialist Republics (USSR). When the USSR collapsed in 1991, the eight gained their independence. They are Armenia, Azerbaijan and Georgia (all west of the Caspian Sea) and five central Asian 'stans': Kazakhstan, Kyrgyzstan, Tajikistan, Turkmenistan and Uzbekistan. Some, like Georgia and Armenia, were ancient nations regaining their freedom. Others, like Kyrgyzstan and Tajikistan, were more recent creations.

GEOGRAPHY

Seven of the eight countries are landlocked,

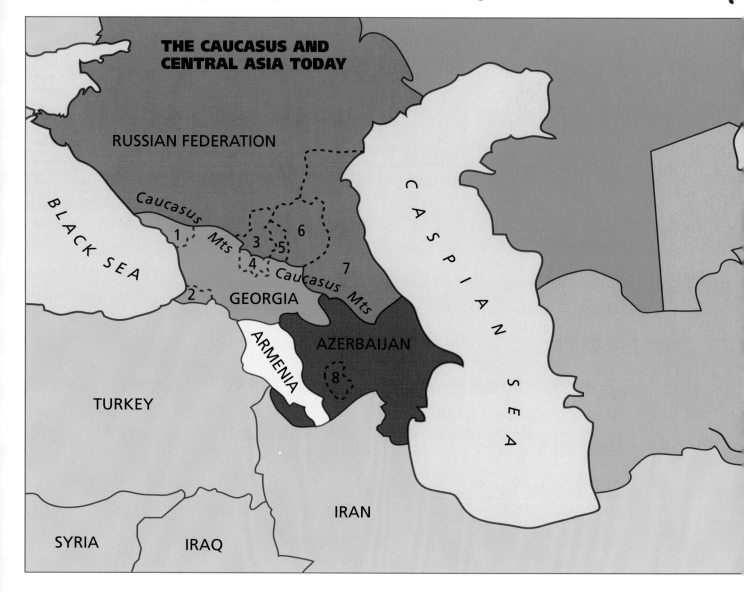

THE CAUCASUS AND CENTRAL ASIA TODAY

RUSSIAN FEDERATION

BLACK SEA

Caucasus Mts

1 3 5 6

4 7

Caucasus Mts

GEORGIA

ARMENIA

AZERBAIJAN

8

CASPIAN SEA

TURKEY

IRAN

SYRIA   IRAQ

although three of them do border the inland Caspian Sea. Only Georgia has a sea coast, on the eastern edge of the Black Sea. Their terrain is mostly mountainous: the Caucasus mountains dominate the three western states, while the Tien Shan and Pamir mountains run through the eastern ones. Deserts and grassy steppes cover Turkmenistan, western Uzbekistan and Kazakhstan.

The five eastern states and Azerbaijan are all part of Asia. Georgia and Armenia are often considered part of Europe, largely because both are Christian rather than Muslim, but geographically both states are part of Asia.

POLITICS

Politically, the eight nations are in a very dangerous, unstable part of the world. The rise of Islamic fundamentalism throughout the Middle East has led to political tensions in the region. Events in neighbouring war-torn Afghanistan have drawn in many of the surrounding countries. Civil wars, boundary disputes and ethnic divisions all add to the ever-present dangers. But the states around the Caspian Sea have some of the biggest oil and natural gas reserves in the world, which are hugely attractive to oil-hungry nations such as the United States and China. These reserves have led to disputes about how such vast resources can best be exploited.

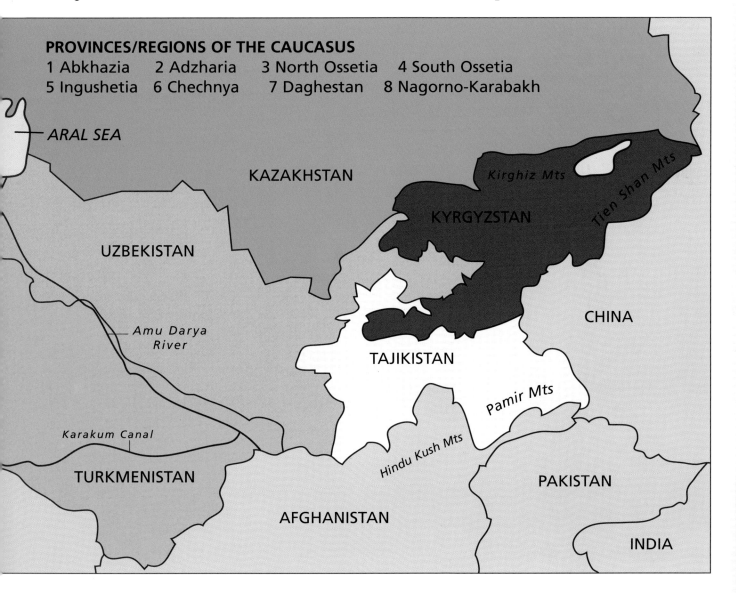

PROVINCES/REGIONS OF THE CAUCASUS
1 Abkhazia 2 Adzharia 3 North Ossetia 4 South Ossetia
5 Ingushetia 6 Chechnya 7 Daghestan 8 Nagorno-Karabakh

THE CAUCASUS

The three Caucasian republics of Armenia, Azerbaijan and Georgia have been fought over and conquered by many powerful neighbours for centuries. But their remoteness has also given them long periods of independence.

ARMENIA

According to tradition, a descendant of the Biblical Noah, called Haig, founded the kingdom of Armenia in the region of Lake Van, in what is now modern-day Turkey. In fact, the first Armenians moved into the region from the Euphrates river valley (in what is now Iraq) around the 8th century BC.

Two centuries later they had set up their own independent kingdom. Subsequently conquered by both the Persians and Alexander the Great, Armenia briefly became independent in 189 BC. It fell under Roman rule a century later.

At the end of the 3rd century AD, Armenia became the first nation in the world to adopt Christianity as its official religion. The country was soon divided between the Roman and Persian Sasanid empires. It was later invaded by the

AZERBAIJAN

The historic region of Azerbaijan extends along the western and southern shores of the Caspian Sea, including the entire coastal region of what is now Iran. Part of the ancient Persian empire – the Persian religious teacher and prophet Zoroaster (Zarathustra) was born here around 1200 BC – Azerbaijan was conquered by Alexander the Great in 328 BC before coming under Persian rule again in AD 226. Unlike both Georgia and Armenia, Azerbaijan was never an independent kingdom, nor did it become Christian: its people converted to Islam after the Arab invasion of the 650s. Later conquered by the Seljuk Turks, Mongols and Tamerlane, Azerbaijan reverted to Persian rule in the 1500s. For the next century, the region was disputed between the Persian and Ottoman empires. Abbas I, Shah of Persia, gained full control in 1603.

Echmiadzin Cathedral in Armenia, seat of the Catholicus or head of the Armenian Church.

Byzantines, Arabs, Seljuk Turks and Mongols. In the 1550s the Ottomans conquered Armenia. Under Ottoman rule, Christian Armenians were persecuted, but they still played a major economic role as merchants and bankers.

GEORGIA

The kingdom of Georgia emerged as an independent state in the 4th century BC. It survived until the Sasanids conquered it in the 3rd century AD. The Sasanids were expelled around AD 400, but the country soon fell under Armenian control. By this time, the Georgians had become Christian, although the arrival of Islam during the 650s isolated both Georgia and Armenia from the Christian states to their west. During the 1000s, King David II united the country and re-established its independence. Later, under Queen Thamar (reigned 1184-1213), Georgia controlled the whole of the Caucasus, and its poets and writers produced its greatest national literature.

Attacked and destroyed by the Mongol warrior Genghis Khan in 1223, the country was again ravaged by Tamerlane - the last Mongol warlord - in the late 1300s. During the mid-1550s, King Alexander I divided the country between his three sons. In 1555

western Georgia (Imertia) fell under Ottoman Turkish rule, and eastern Georgia (Kakhetia and Karthlia) under Persian rule.

Genghis Khan (c.1162–1227) founded the Mongol Empire that stretched from China to the Black Sea.

THE CAUCASUS

500s BC Armenia emerges as an independent kingdom in what is now eastern Turkey

331-328 Alexander the Great conquers Armenia and Azerbaijan

300s Georgia emerges as an independent kingdom

189–67 Brief period of Armenian independence before conquest by Romans

AD 200s Persian Sasanid empire controls Azerbaijan and Georgia

c290 Armenia becomes world's first Christian nation

387 Armenia divided between Roman and Sasanid empires

400s Georgia becomes Christian

650s Azerbaijan becomes Muslim

1200s Georgia dominates Caucasus

1220s Mongols invade and ransack the region

1386–94 Mongol armies of Tamerlane sweep through Caucasus

1550s Ottomans conquer whole of Armenia

1555 Georgia divided between Persian and Ottoman empires

1603 Azerbaijan under Persian rule

CENTRAL ASIA

The five central Asian republics lie on one of the world's major crossroads. Traders travelling between Europe and eastern Asia, armies conquering new lands and nomads in search of fertile pastures, have all passed through this region over the centuries.

THE SILK ROAD

The first people to live in central Asia were nomads, who roamed with their flocks in search of good pasture and fresh water. The land they occupied lay between the great civilisations of China to the east and Persia, Greece and, later, Rome to the west. Trade between these empires was carried out along the Silk Road, a route that stretched from the old Chinese capital of Chang'an (now Xi'an) over the Pamirs and into central Asia. There the Silk Road crossed Persia, and reached the eastern Mediterranean coastline.

The Silk Road was established in about 600 BC. It flourished until the Roman and other empires fell apart, after the 3rd century AD.

NAMING THE REGION

When Alexander the Great and his Macedonian army invaded Central Asia in 329 BC, his army crossed a river they called the Oxus. Scholars of ancient history called the region Transoxania (or Transoxiania), because it lay across the river from Persia and the rest of the civilised world. The Persians and Arabs called the river the Jaihun, and in the biblical Book of Genesis the Jaihun (or Gihon) is the second river created by God to flow from Paradise. Today the river is called the Amu Darya. During the 8th century AD, when the Arabs invaded Transoxania, Turkic nomads lived in the area. So the Arabs named it Bilad al-Turk, 'Land of the Turks' or 'Turkestan', a name used until 1924.

Silks, ivories, glass and other precious goods were traded for gold, silver and other items. The merchants of central Asia created great cities, such as Samarkand and Bukhara.

The ancient Silk Road, along which traders have travelled for more than 2,000 years.

THE ARAB INVASIONS

The first people in the region spoke Farsi (Persian), but Turkic speakers from the steppes of northern China gradually displaced them. During the 3rd century BC, monks from India brought Buddhism to the area, but many nomads stayed loyal to the ancient Persian religion of Zoroastrianism.

From about 650 onwards, Arab raiders began to cross the Amu Darya, bringing their new religion of Islam with them. A century later, the whole region was Muslim, and the Arab language and written script were in use. From then on, successive Islamic empires dominated the region.

The Registan of Samarkand, the 15th-century heart of Tamerlane's capital city.

THE MONGOLS

In 1219 the Mongol armies of Genghis Khan swept in from the steppes of eastern Asia. At his death in 1227, Genghis Khan ruled an empire that stretched from eastern China to the Black Sea. His successors extended the empire further into eastern Europe, but it was too big for one ruler to control. In 1259 the western part of the empire was divided in three - the Chagatai Khanate of central Asia, the Khanate of the Golden Horde in southern Russia and the southern Ilkhanate in Persia.

The Golden Horde and Chagatai Khanates survived for several centuries, but the Ilkhanate collapsed during the 1330s. It was eventually conquered by Tamerlane, the Mongol warrior and Muslim emir of Samarkand, whose empire stretched from the Black Sea to India. After he died, however, his empire slowly fell apart.

CENTRAL ASIA

700s BC Persian-speaking nomads move into central Asia

329 Alexander the Great invades

200 BC–AD 200 Silk Road flourishes

600 Turkic speakers dominate region from Mongolia to the Aral Sea

c650 Arab raiders introduce Islam to region

751 Arab armies defeat invading Chinese at battle of the Talas River

763 Abbasid caliphate rules region from Baghdad

1037 Seljuk Turks begin to conquer region

1229 Mongol armies of Genghis Khan invade

1259 After death of Great Khan Möngke, central Asia divided into three separate khanates

1280 The khanate of

the Golden Horde adopts Turkish as its official language

1300 Most Mongols have converted to Islam

1361–1405 Tamerlane establishes Timurid Empire

1502 Golden Horde khanate collapses

13

THE COMING OF THE RUSSIANS

During the 19th century, the countries of the Caucasus and central Asia were gradually taken over by the Russian Empire. They were to remain under Russian control for almost two centuries.

RUSSIAN EXPANSION

In 1480 the Grand Duchy of Muscovy, a small landlocked state in north-east Europe, declared its independence from Mongol rule. It then expanded its territory. Over the next 400 years, Russia - as Muscovy was called by the late 1600s - pushed its borders west towards the Baltic Sea, south towards the Black Sea and east across Siberia to the Pacific Ocean. As it did so, Russia came into conflict with its powerful neighbours, such as the Ottoman Empire.

THE CAUCASUS

By the 1780s the Russian Empire extended as far as the Caucasus. The Ottoman and Persian empires had divided Georgia between them since 1555, although each part was semi-independent. In 1783 the king of Persian-ruled eastern Georgia tried to unite the country, but he was faced with opposition from both the Ottomans and Persians. He signed a treaty of alliance with Russia, and recognised its supremacy. In 1801 the last eastern king, George XIII, gave his country over to Russian control. Western Georgia was soon captured from the Ottomans by the Russians.

Azerbaijan, briefly under Russian control from 1723-32, was finally acquired from Persia by 1828. So too was Armenia,

ALEXANDER II

Tsar Alexander II of Russia (reigned 1855–81), the 'Tsar Liberator', emancipated (freed) millions of serfs in 1861 and freed Bulgaria from Turkish rule in 1878. During his reign, Russian control was extended throughout the Caucasus when the Chechens were finally overcome in 1859, and across central Asia, where most of the Muslim emirates were absorbed into the Russian Empire, as well as extensive gains in the Far East. At home, he made huge attempts to modernise Russian social and political life, introducing universal military service, reforming local government and the judicial system, including introducing trial by jury, and attempting to reform Russia's chaotic finances. Opposed by both conservatives and revolutionaries, he was assassinated in 1881 by the terrorist *Narodnaia Volia* (People's Will) group.

A wealthy 19th-century merchant of Bukhara.

although a large part of it stayed within the Ottoman Empire. In 1878 Russian-held Georgia and Armenia regained more of their historic land when Russia defeated the Ottoman Empire in battle.

CENTRAL ASIA

The Mongol khanates and Tamerlane's empire slowly collapsed after 1500 but some independent Muslim emirates and khanates flourished, especially those at Bukhara, Khiva and Kokand (all now in Uzbekistan). These states were, however, at the mercy of their neighbours. Nadir Shah of Persia conquered the southern khanates during the 1740s, while Manchu-ruled China occupied the eastern khanates by the 1780s. In the 19th century, however, both these empires were pushed out of central Asia by the ever-expanding Russian empire. By 1884 Russia had occupied the remaining khanates.

UNDER RUSSIAN CONTROL

1740–47 Nadir Shah of Persia invades lands around the eastern Caspian Sea

1783 Manchu China conquers what is now eastern Kazakhstan

1783 King of eastern Georgia accepts Russian supremacy in return for assistance

1801 Last king of eastern Georgia abdicates and unites kingdom with Russia

1803–29 Western Georgia acquired

1805–28 Azerbaijan acquired from Persia

1828 Armenia acquired from Persia

1822–65 Russian Empire occupies northern Kazakh khanates, and conquest completed with the capture of city of Tashkent

1868–76 Emirate of Bukhara and khanates of Khiva and Kokand conquered

1878 Georgia and Armenia increase size after Ottoman defeat

1881 Russians crush Turkmen resistance at battle of Göktepe

1884 Russian Empire completes conquest of southern khanates with acquisition of city of Merv

THE GREAT GAME

As the Russian Empire expanded into central Asia, it approached the borders of another great empire, that of the British in India. For almost a century the two empires fought a shadowy conflict, that became known as the 'Great Game'.

THE BRITISH IN INDIA

The British had been in India since the mid-1600s, when the East India Company of traders had concentrated its activities on India. By 1800 Britain had become the leading commercial and colonial power on the Indian subcontinent.

At this time, the borders of Russia were more than 3,000 kilometres away from the British in India. But in 1807 Emperor Napoleon of France suggested a joint invasion of India to the Russian tsar, with the purpose of weakening British power.

The threat of invasion came to nothing, but the British were worried. They became more alarmed when the expanding Russian Empire occupied central Asia. Russia was growing steadily, as it had done for 300 years, at the rate of 142 square kilometres a day and 52,000 square kilometres a year. This brought Russia ever closer to India, threatening the British, who extended their rule over more of India in response. But this action alarmed the Russians, who feared that the British would stir up their new Muslim subjects against them. By the 1860s, the 'Great Game' was well under way.

This engraving shows British forces during the First Anglo-Afghan War of 1839-42, in which the occupation of Afghanistan ended in a humiliating defeat for the British.

PLAYING THE GAME

The British twice invaded Afghanistan, which was strategically important to the defence of India, but they failed to subdue this mountainous country. By 1880 the Russians controlled most of central Asia, and both sides were sending out spies to see what the other side was doing. An agreement between the two empires defined the border between Russia and Afghanistan, but further Russian advances in 1884 alarmed the British.

In 1891 Russian troops pushed east across the Pamir Mountains to the borders of

The Pamir Mountains formed a natural barrier between the Russian Empire and British India until crossed by Russian forces in 1891.

British-held Kashmir. The two empires were now only 32 kilometres apart. War was possible, but a deal was struck. The frontier between Russian central Asia and eastern Afghanistan was fixed by a thin strip of land, 240 kilometres long and in places no more than 16 kilometres wide, stretching up to the Chinese border. The Wakhan corridor, or 'Afghan finger', separated the two empires, and kept the peace. The 'Great Game' was almost over.

THE GREAT GAME

1807 Emperor Napoleon proposes a French–Russian invasion of British India

1818 British dominate India

1839–42 First Afghan War ends in catastrophe as British troops forced to withdraw

1849 British conquer the Punjab in north-west India

1857 British government takes control of East India Company

1873 First agreement between Britain and Russia to define northern border of Afghanistan

1877 Queen Victoria of Britain becomes empress of India

1878–80 Second Afghan War

1884 Russians complete conquest of central Asia

1891 Russians advance into Pamir Mountains

1893 British fix Afghan–Indian border along the Durand line

1895 Pamir Boundary Commission creates 'Afghan finger'

1907 Anglo–Russian Entente (agreement) settles all existing disputes in Afghanistan, Tibet and Persia

T E GREAT WAR

In July 1914 war broke out in Europe and soon spread around the world. The Great War (as World War I was known at the time) brought the Russian Empire to an end.

FIGHTING IN THE CAUCASUS

In the war, Russia fought alongside Britain and France against Germany, Austria-Hungary and the Ottoman (Turkish) Empire. The Turks attacked Russia's naval bases in the Black Sea and its forces in the Caucasus, but they were heavily defeated in January 1915. Further battles weakened Turkish power in the Caucasus and the Russians captured most of Turkish Armenia during 1916.

THE RUSSIAN REVOLUTION

In March 1917 the situation changed decisively. Revolution broke out in Russia. Independence campaigners in the Caucasus seized their chance, and held elections in Russian Armenia, Georgia and Azerbaijan. On 17 September 1917 the Council of the Transcaucasian Peoples set up the Federal Republic of Transcaucasia. The new republic was split, however, between Georgians who wanted total independence, Armenians who wanted to maintain their links with Russia, and Azerbaijanis who wanted to maintain their links with the Ottoman Empire.

In November 1917 the Bolshevik Party seized power in the second Russian revolution. They set up the world's first communist state. In March 1918 Russia

ARMENIAN GENOCIDE

In the late 19th century, Armenian nationalists campaigned for an independent state in eastern Turkey. They were massacred by Ottoman troops in 1895 and 1909. In April 1915 the Ottoman government accused the 1.75 million Armenians under their control of collaborating with Russia. Over the next seven months, 600,000 Armenians were killed, and 500,000 deported to Mesopotamia (modern-day Iraq), only 90,000 of whom survived. Then 400,000 Russian Armenians were killed when Turkish troops invaded the Caucasus in 1918. The massacres continued until 1922, when the remaining Armenians were driven from Turkey. The atrocities against the Armenians were the first acts of genocide in the 20th century.

A refugee camp for Armenians, shown in 1915.

made peace with its enemies and recognised the independence of the Caucasus (although it gave part of it to Turkey). The treaty caused huge dissent in Transcaucasia, which eventually collapsed. The three states then became independent.

INTERNAL CONFLICT

The next three years were very confusing ones. The three countries fought for their independence against Turkey and Russia,

The Bolshevik Red Army, the strongest force in the Caucasus, seized control of the area by May 1921.

and against each other. Local Bolsheviks seized power in many of the cities, while rival German and British troops also intervened, but the Bolshevik Red Army was the strongest force. It took Azerbaijan in 1920, and Armenia and Georgia by May 1921. The brief period of Caucasian independence was now over.

WAR AND INDEPENDENCE

July 1914 War breaks out in Europe

Oct 1914 Ottoman (Turkish) Empire joins war against Russia

April 1915 Turks begin campaign of genocide against Armenians

March 1917 Revolution in Russia leads to abdication of Tsar Nicholas II

Aug 1917 Elections held to the Council of the Transcaucasian Peoples

Sept 1917 Federal Republic of Transcaucasia established in Tbilisi, Georgia

Nov 1917 Second revolution in Russia brings Bolsheviks to power

Feb 1918 Turkey invades Armenia and Georgia as Russian power collapses

March 1918 Treaty of Brest-Litovsk

May 1918 Azerbaijan sides with Turkey and republic collapses; Georgia and Armenia now independent; German and Turkish troops intervene

Nov 1918 World War I ends: German and Turkish troops replaced by British

April 1920 Red Army seizes Azerbaijan

July 1920 British troops leave Caucasus

May 1921 Red Army ends independence of both Georgia and Armenia

COMMUNIST RULE

When the Bolsheviks seized power in November 1917, anti-Bolsheviks tried to regain control and civil war broke out. Many regions declared independence. By 1921 the Bolsheviks had won, and many years of repressive, brutal rule followed.

THE NEW ORDER

In 1922 the Russian government restructured its territories as the Union of the Soviet Socialist Republics (USSR). The different regions were united within a federal republic. In the Caucasus region Armenia, Azerbaijan and Georgia were again merged into a Transcaucasian Soviet Socialist Federal Republic. In 1936 the three countries became separate republics once again, this time within the USSR.

In central Asia, Islamic rebels, called *basmachi* (bandits) by the Russians, fought for independence. From 1921 they were led by Enver Pasha, the Ottoman Empire's war minister, who had fled his Turkish homeland when his country was defeated in 1918. Pasha convinced Lenin, the Russian leader, that he could control the area on Russia's behalf. But once there Pasha switched sides and fought the Red Army, until he was finally defeated outside Bukhara in 1922. The basmachi fought on until the 1930s, but the old order was swept away. Four socialist republics replaced the emirates that had survived under tsarist rule. In 1924 these were reorganised into five republics based on their different peoples. All eventually become full members of the USSR. By1936, the modern map of the eight Caucasus and central Asian states was settled.

COMMUNIST RULE

Communist rule extended to every aspect of life. Religion was suppressed, Islamic law banned and political opposition crushed. 'Enemies of the state' were killed or exiled to Siberia. Private property was abolished, industries controlled by the state and farms were merged into huge collectives.

Under communism, vast public works programmes were undertaken throughout central Asia.

The communists believed that everyone had the right to an education, so many new schools and colleges were built. In central Asia, six new written languages based on local dialects replaced the old Turkic or Farsi languages. At first these new languages were written in Arabic, but in 1928 they changed to the Roman alphabet (used in this book). Later, the Russian Cyrillic alphabet was imposed. Throughout the eight republics, Russian

ENFORCING COMMUNISM

Resistance to communism in the Caucasus continued long after the Bolshevik victory. An anti-communist uprising broke out in Georgia in 1924 (and again in 1956), while in 1929 the Chechens of the northern Caucasus rose up against the imposition of collective farms. Across the Caucasus many thousands were killed or deported in the 'show trials' of the 1930s: 14,000 Chechens and Ingush were arrested on 31 July 1937 alone. In June 1941 the armies of Nazi Germany invaded the USSR and advanced towards the Caucasus. In response, Stalin accused some 5 million Soviet citizens from 50 different nationalities of collaboration. He moved entire populations east to central Asia or Siberia. Tatars from Crimea, Germans from the Volga region and Chechens and Ingush were all transported. Half the 478,479 Chechens and Ingush who were deported in 1944 lost their lives, while those who survived were not allowed to return to their homes until 1957.

Joseph Stalin (1897–1953) leader of the USSR.

'For twenty years now, the Soviet authorities have been fighting my people, aiming to destroy them group by group. The real object of this war [against us] is the annihilation of our nation as a whole.'

Hassan Israilov, Chechen rebel fighter, 1940

became the first language, and Russians held all positions of power. In theory the USSR consisted of 15 individual republics; in reality, power lay with the Communist Party in Moscow. Its leader, Joseph Stalin, ruled the country as a virtual dictator from 1924 until his death in 1953.

SOVIET RULE

Nov 1917 Bolsheviks take power and Lenin leads Russia

1920 Khanate of Khiva and Emirate of Bukhara replaced by People's Soviet Republics; autonomous republics set up in Turkestan and Kazakhstan

Mar 1921 Bolshevik victory

March 1922 Transcaucasian Soviet Socialist Federal Republic set up

Aug 1922 Enver Pasha killed but basmachi revolt continues until early 1930s

Dec 1922 Union of the Soviet Socialist Republics (USSR) created

1924 Lenin dies; Stalin is new leader

1924 Central Asia becomes two republics: Uzbekistan and Turkmenistan, and three autonomous regions: Tajikistan, Kazakhstan, Kyrgyzstan

1929 Tajikistan becomes full republic of USSR, followed by

Kazakhstan and Kyrgyzstan in 1936

1936 Georgia, Armenia, and Azerbaijan independent republics within USSR

Feb 1944 Entire Chechen and Ingush populations shipped to Kazakhstan

1953 Death of Stalin

INDEPENDENCE

In 1985 a new leader took power in the USSR and pledged reforms. But within six years, the USSR itself had disappeared, and its eight Caucasian and Asian republics then became fully independent nations.

REFORMING THE SYSTEM

When Mikhail Gorbachev became leader of the USSR in 1985 he knew that it had serious economic, social and military problems. Gorbachev tried to address these problems through reforms of the entire Soviet structure, but he wanted to keep the existing communist system, rather than replace it with something else.

> **'We had to change everything.'**
>
> **Mikhail Gorbachev, 1991**

One of the main problems he faced was corruption. Since the 1970s, the communist boss of Uzbekistan had made himself rich by claiming vast amounts of money from the central government for cotton - the republic's main crop - that was never grown. He used the money to bribe government ministers and local officials, giving them bags stuffed full of money to keep quiet. In Kazakhstan the entire Communist Party was corrupt, with officials of all ranks enjoying free holidays and other luxury gifts.

Gorbachev began to tackle these problems. In 1986 he sent in a Russian to clean up Kazakhstan, but anti-Russian riots broke out in the country and in 1989 he was forced to back down. By now, racial and ethnic tensions had risen across the USSR. Racial riots broke out in Kyrgyzstan, Uzbekistan and Georgia, and in January

MIKHAIL GORBACHEV

Mikhail Gorbachev (b.1931) studied law at Moscow University before joining the Communist Party in 1952. He quickly rose through the party, making a name for himself as a reformer, and became leader in 1985. He embarked on a rapid programme of social reform, got rid of hard-line communists from his government in 1988, and rewrote the Soviet constitution to allow non-communists to stand for the duma (parliament). In 1989 he was elected president of the USSR but he was unable to retain control of the country. He resigned as president when the USSR finally collapsed in 1991.

1990 Soviet troops fired on demonstrators in Baku, capital of Azerbaijan, which had just declared war on its neighbouring republic of Armenia (see pp 28-29).

INDEPENDENCE

Gorbachev tried to hold the USSR together by giving greater power to the republics. This policy was overwhelmingly approved in a referendum in March 1991, but by this time nationalists in many republics wanted full independence. The Baltic republic of Lithuania had already left and Georgia was about to, but the rest waited until after August 1991, when hard-line communists staged a coup against Gorbachev.

Although the coup failed, Gorbachev was

Georgian discontent with Soviet rule erupted onto the streets in 1990. Thousands demonstrated in favour of independence. Georgia became an independent republic on 26 May 1991.

politically weakened by it. The remaining 13 republics soon declared their independence while three of them - Russia, Belarus and Ukraine - set up a new, loose organisation called the Commonwealth of Independent States (CIS) to replace the USSR. With no country to lead, Gorbachev finally resigned as president. The eight Caucasian and central Asian republics were now on their own.

THE END OF SOVIET RULE

March 1985 Mikhail Gorbachev leads USSR

Dec 1986 Gorbachev's reforms in Kazakhstan met with riots

Jan 1990 Soviet troops fire on demonstrators in Baku, Azerbaijan

March 1990 Lithuania declares its independence

June 1990 Ethnic riots in Kyrgyzstan

17 March 1991 Referendum approves Gorbachev's plans to reform USSR

26 May 1991 Georgia declares its independence

19-21 Aug 1991 Coup against Gorbachev fails

30–31 Aug 1991 Azerbaijan (30th), Kyrgyzstan and Uzbekistan (31st) all declare independence

9 Sept 1991 Tajikistan declares independence, followed by Armenia (21st) and

Turkmenistan (27 October)

8 Dec 1991 Russia, Belarus, Ukraine set up Commonwealth of Independent States

16 Dec 1991 Kazakhstan leaves USSR

25 Dec 1991 Gorbachev resigns as president

CHECHEN FREEDOM

The Russian Federation, made up of many different republics, emerged after the USSR broke up. One of these republics, Chechnya, then fought a bitter war for its own independence.

RUSSIAN RULE

The Russian Federation consists of 89 republics, regions and other districts. Most of these are based around different national homelands and enjoy various degrees of self-government. Most of them have no wish to leave the federation. Chechnya, however, has bitterly resented Russian control ever since it was finally conquered in 1859.

The mountainous republic of Chechnya lies on the north side of the Caucasus. Its people are Muslim, speak their own language and are quite separate from the Russians who have tried to rule them for the past 200 years.

During Russian and Soviet rule, the Chechens have fought hard for independence.

THE FIGHT FOR INDEPENDENCE

In the chaos surrounding the break-up of the USSR, Chechen leaders declared independence. At first the Russian government negotiated with them, but fighting broke out when Chechens opposed to independence tried to capture the capital, Grozny. Russia then began direct military action, bombing Grozny with great ferocity. Russian troops occupied Grozny in early 1995, but Chechen fighters took to the mountains and started a

The Chechen capital Grozny in 1999, largely reduced to rubble after five years of fighting.

guerrilla war. They even carried out successful raids into Russian territory. In 1996 the Chechen leader, Dzhokhar Dudayev, a former Soviet air force pilot, was killed. The two sides reached an agreement to end the conflict and stopped fighting. Russia agreed to withdraw its troops, but agreement on the future status of Chechnya was postponed.

Chechen leader Dzhokhar Dudayev, who was killed in 1996.

THE FIGHT GOES ON

The conflict resumed in 1999, when Chechen separatists attacked villages in neighbouring Daghestan. Apartments across Russia were bombed, killing 300 people. Many people suspected the FSB (Russian

THE 'MOUNTAINEERS'

Although the Russian Empire acquired most of the Caucasus region after Georgia joined the empire in 1801, Chechnya remained independent, and Russian troops were unable to control the rebellious mountain-dwellers. In 1818 General Yermolov, sent to control the Chechens, built a fort in northern Chechnya. He named it *grozny*, which means 'threatening' or 'menacing' in Russian. It was joined by more forts, built to subdue the country. But the Chechens refused to join Russia, and fought a long war, from 1828 to 1859, until they were finally subdued. They rebelled in 1877–78, and again in May 1918, when they declared an independent North Caucasus Mountain Republic. The Red Army subdued them in 1921, but a Chechen republic existed briefly within the Russian Republic from 1936–46.

secret service) of planting the bombs, however, because the Russian military and security services had never accepted defeat in Chechnya. After Vladimir Putin became president, the war intensified. When the World Trade Center was attacked in 2001, Putin used this opportunity to brand all Chechens as terrorists. He has pursued a ruthless war against them ever since. The Chechens have taken hostages and planted bombs in Moscow, and other cities. Both sides have suffered huge casualties.

THE STRUGGLE FOR INDEPENDENT CHECHNYA

1918 Chechens declare independence

1921 Chechen independence ended by Red Army

1936–46 Chechen-Ingush Autonomous Soviet Socialist Republic created

1944 387,229 Chechens (and 91,250 Ingush) deported to central Asia

Nov 1991 Chechnya declares independence

Feb 1994 Civil war breaks out between pro- and anti-independence sides

Dec 1994 Russian troops invade Chechnya and take city of Grozny

Dec 1995 Chechens turn down Russian offer of autonomy

Aug 1996 Peace terms agreed

Sept 1999 Mysterious bombs kill 300 across Russia

Oct 1999 Russian troops invade Chechnya again

Oct 2002 Chechen rebels hold 800 people hostage in Moscow theatre; 120 hostages killed when troops storm building

May 2004 Pro-Russian Chechen leader Akhmad Kadyrov killed in bomb attack

GEORGIA IN TURMOIL

Ever since it gained independence in 1991, Georgia - the westernmost republic in the Caucasus - has endured many years of civil war and political turmoil.

Soviet-era tower blocks dominate the skyline of Tbilisi, the Georgian capital.

AN OLD AND NEW NATION

Although Georgia joined Russia voluntarily in 1801, it retained its own identity and was proud of its distinct history and culture. Nationalists always longed for Georgia to be independent once again, and when the USSR broke up they elected Zviad Gamsakhurdia as their leader. In May 1991 Georgia declared independence, the second Soviet republic (after Lithuania) to do so.

The new republic faced immediate problems. Political groups opposed to Gamsakhurdia rebelled. The South Ossetia region wanted to join the Russian republic of North Ossetia, and Abkhazia wanted independence. Both received arms and support from Russia. The southern region of Adzharia also wanted independence. Gamsakhurdia failed to unify the country, and he fled into exile in 1992. An interim government was formed, but the chaos continued when Gamsakhurdia returned in 1993 to fight for the presidency. This time, however, he was unsuccessful.

FACT FILE: GEORGIA

Capital: Tbilisi
Population: 5.2 million
People: Georgian 70%, Armenian 8%, Azeri 6%, Russian 6%, Ossetian 3%, Other 7%
Languages: Georgian, Russian, Abkhazian
Religions: Georgian, Russian or Armenian Orthodox Christian, Muslim

THE RUSSIANS RETURN

The new president, Eduard Shevardnadze, was faced with war on three fronts, and reluctantly asked for help from Russia. The rebellions were suppressed, and in return Georgia joined the Russian-led CIS. However, this left Georgia with unwelcome Russian troops in its country, and with two regions still wishing to leave. The problem of South Ossetia was partially settled in 1996, but Abkhazia refused to recognise Georgian control. To add to the problems, Russia accused Georgia of sheltering Chechen rebels in the remote Pankisi Gorge, and threatened to invade if they were not dealt with. This situation was defused, but relations between the two countries remain tense.

CORRUPT GOVERNMENT

Shevardnadze had been a good diplomat, but he was a weak president. The economy collapsed, and corruption and crime flourished. In 2003 opponents accused him of rigging elections, and mass demonstrations forced him to resign in the so-called 'Velvet Revolution'. His successor, Mikhail Saakashvili, won an overwhelming election victory. He promised to ally Georgia with Europe and perhaps even to join the European Union, which would reduce Russian influence in the country.

EDUARD SHEVARDNADZE

Eduard Shevardnadze was born in Georgia in 1928 and joined the USSR's Communist Party in 1948. He rose through its ranks to become a Georgian government minister in 1968 and party leader in 1972. In 1985 Mikhail Gorbachev chose him to be the Soviet Foreign Minister. Shevardnadze helped push through many significant reforms, but in November 1990 he resigned as foreign minister in protest at the weakness of Gorbachev's government. He briefly returned to the job after the failed August 1991 coup against Gorbachev, and remained until the collapse of the USSR in December 1991. He was president of Georgia from 1992, but was forced from office in 2003.

GEORGIA

Mar 1990 Georgia declares 1922 union with USSR illegal

May 1991 Independence; Gamsakhurdia elected president

Nov 1991 South Ossetia fights to join Russian North Ossetia

Jan 1992 Gamsakhurdia flees country; interim government set up

June 1992 Ceasefire in South Ossetia

July 1992 Abhkazia declares its independence

Oct 1992 Shevardnadze elected president of Georgia

Sep 1993 Gamsakhurdia returns to lead rebellion

Oct 1993 Georgia is last former Soviet republic to join CIS

May 1994 Georgia and Abkhazia agree ceasefire

April 1996 Georgia and South Ossetia settle differences

Sep 2002 Russia threatens to invade to remove Chechen rebels

Nov 2003 Shevardnadze forced out

Jan 2004 Mikhail Saakashvili elected president

May 2004 Georgia takes full control of rebel Adzharia province

The recent history of both Armenia and Azerbaijan has been dominated by tension and conflict over disputed territory. One look at the map makes the reasons clear.

DISPUTED LANDS

Armenia and Azerbaijan are both fiercely nationalist. Armenia, the smallest Soviet republic, has always had to fight for its independence: it is a Christian nation surrounded on three sides by Muslim nations. Azerbaijan was the first republic that tried to leave the USSR. In January 1990 - almost two years before the USSR collapsed - the Azeri Popular Front defeated the Communist Party and declared independence. Soviet forces crushed the rebellion and reinstated the communist government, which itself declared independence when the USSR fell apart.

Both Armenia and Azerbaijan once extended far beyond their current borders. Millions of Armenians lived in what is now Turkey before the genocide of 1915-22, and there are more Azeris in neighbouring Iran than in Azerbaijan itself. The border between the two countries is very muddled, with enclaves of one country buried inside the other. The enclave of Nagorno-Karabakh is officially part of Azerbaijan, but it is populated almost entirely by Armenians.

DISPUTED ENCLAVES

The conflict over Nagorno-Karabakh dates back to 1922, when Stalin gave the enclave to Azerbaijan despite claims that it was historically part of Armenia. Fighting broke out in 1988, when ethnic Armenians in Nagorno-Karabakh demanded unification with Armenia.

FACT FILE: ARMENIA

Capital: Yerevan
Population: 3.8 million
People: Armenian 93%, Azeri 3% Russian 2%, Other 2%
Languages: Armenian, Russian
Religion: Armenian Orthodox Christian

FACT FILE: AZERBAIJAN

Capital: Baku
Population: 8.1 million
People: Azeri 90%, Russian 3%, Daghenstani 3%, Armenian 2%, Other 2%
Languages: Azerbaijani, Russian
Religion: Shi'a Muslim

Armenian militia fight to unify Nagorno-Karabakh with the rest of Armenia.

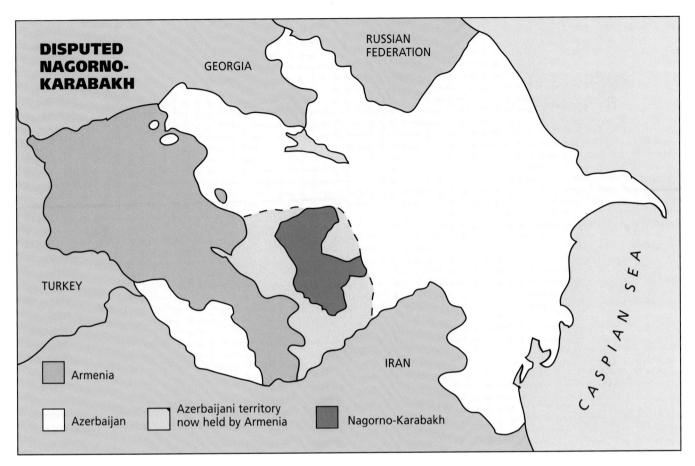

They clashed with Soviet Azeri forces, and this intensified in 1990 when Azerbaijan briefly declared war on Armenia over the issue.

In 1992, Armenian Nagorno-Karabakh forces managed to form a land bridge with Armenia. By the end of 1993, Nagorno-Karabakh forces occupied the entire enclave. They also held all Azerbaijani territory separating the enclave from Armenia and

the surrounding mountains: about 15% of all the Azeri territory. Thousands died or fled the violence as refugees.

A ceasefire was agreed in 1994, but fighting began again after the region declared independence in 1996. Both sides are committed to a peaceful solution, but talks between the two countries in recent years have failed to break the deadlock. It remains an area of tension and danger.

ARMENIA AND AZERBAIJAN

Feb 1988 Regional parliament in Nagorno-Karabakh votes to join Armenia, leading to ethnic violence in both countries

Jan 1990 Azeri Popular Front declares both independence and war on Armenia, but revolt is crushed by Soviet

troops and peace restored

Aug 1991 Azerbaijan independent

Sept 1991 Armenia independent

May 1992 Nagorno-Karabakh fights for unification with Armenia

June 1993 Heydar Aliev becomes president of Azerbaijan

May 1994 Ceasefire agreed

1996 Nagorno-Karabakh declares independence, which is not recognised by Armenia or Azerbaijan

Apr–May 1997 Renewed border conflict

Oct 1997 Both sides agree to seek peaceful solution to conflict

Mar-Apr 2001 Presidents of both nations fail to reach agreement

THE IMPACT OF AFGHANISTAN

For the past 30 years, the mountainous state of Afghanistan has been devastated by conflict. Events here have had a profound effect throughout central Asia.

THE CONFLICT BEGINS

The civil war in Afghanistan began in 1975, when Islamic leaders who opposed the modernising government of Muhammad Daoud fled to Pakistan, and set up the Mujahideen ('holy warriors') to fight it. Daoud was assassinated in 1978, and this led to the establishment of a Soviet-backed communist government.

In the turmoil that followed, the United States ambassador was killed. The USA blamed the new government, and began to fund the Mujahideen. The USSR, fearing American influence, then occupied the country, starting a long and bloody war.

THE TALIBAN

The USSR withdrew in 1989 and the communist president lost control to the Mujahideen, who then argued among themselves. As a result, the Taliban took power (see right), as the most likely guarantee of order in the country. But the four main Mujahideen groups formed the Northern Alliance and continued their fight for power in Afghanistan.

After the 2001 terrorist attacks on the USA, the Taliban was accused of sheltering al-Qaida and its leader, Osama Bin Laden. American troops invaded and, with the Northern Alliance, overthrew the Taliban.

Soviet troops occupied Afghanistan from 1979 until 1988.

THE TALIBAN

Mullah Muhammad Omar, a Muslim cleric from Kandahar in southern Afghanistan, formed the Taliban in the early 1990s. He believed in a strict interpretation of *Shar'ia* (Islamic law). Men were forbidden to shave, and women could not go to school, or work outside the home. Television, radio and even music were all banned. Most Taliban members came from the majority Pashtun tribe of Afghanistan, its traditional rulers, and they could unite the country in a way the minority Tajik- and Uzbek-dominated Mujahideen and Northern Alliance could not. Above all, the Taliban offered order and security to a country devastated by war since 1975. They gained widespread support from war-weary Afghans.

Under Taliban rule, all women had to wear a burka.

THE AFGHAN EFFECT

This lengthy civil war has had a dramatic effect in central Asia. After 1979, Afghanistan became a battleground between the communist USSR and capitalist USA. Arms and money poured into the country, but neither superpower won over the Afghan people, who increasingly turned to fundamentalist Islam in response to outside interference. The development of a newly militant Islam has created great instability throughout the region. Islamic rebels, inspired by the Taliban and equipped with Afghan weapons, have brought chaos to Kyrgyzstan, Tajikistan and Uzbekistan. They have also trafficked in drugs to raise money: Afghanistan is the world's major producer of opium poppies, the raw material for heroin. The arrival of American troops in the region has added to this explosive mixture.

AFGHANISTAN

1919 Afghan independence recognised

July 1973 King Zahir Shah overthrown and republic established under Daoud

1975 Islamic revolt led by Mujahideen begins

Apr 1978 Daoud assassinated; communists take over

Feb 1979 American ambassador killed

July 1979 USA starts to arm Mujahideen opposition

Dec 1979 80,000 Soviet troops occupy country

Feb 1989 Last Soviet troops leave country

Apr 1992 Najibullah loses control to

Mujahideen; Islamic Republic set up

Dec 1992 Civil war between Mujahideen groups begins

Sept 1996 Taliban take Kabul, the capital; four Mujahideen groups form Northern Alliance to fight Taliban

Sept 2001 al-Qaida terrorist attacks on

targets in the USA on 11 September

Oct 2001 US planes bomb Afghanistan; Taliban overthrown

June 2002 Hamid Karzai appointed head of state

Jan 2004 New democratic constitution is agreed

31

These two easternmost, mountainous republics of central Asia are the poorest of the former Soviet Asian republics. Both are torn by ethnic conflicts.

TAJIKISTAN

The people of Tajikistan, unlike their Turkic neighbours, are mainly of Persian (Iranian) origin. They speak a language closely related to the Farsi spoken in Iran, although it is still written in Cyrillic script. The Tajiks form a majority, but there is a lot of ethnic tension with the large Uzbek minority, which led to open conflict in 1998. The Russians who moved here during Soviet rule are discriminated against, as they are in neighbouring Uzbekistan. The Russian population has halved to about 200,000 since independence.

Tajikistan is the only former Soviet Asian republic to have endured civil war. The Communist Party won the first post-independence election, but opposition parties were excluded and civil war broke out. Rival groups fought for power, and the Islamic Renaissance Party fought to set up an Islamic republic. The new communist president, Rakhmanov, received Russian help because of fears that a fundamentalist state would emerge in the region. In 1997 a ceasefire was agreed but Russian military support stayed to help keep the peace. It is still there.

FACT FILE: TAJIKISTAN

Capital: **Dushanbe**
Population: **6.1 million**
People: **Tajik 65%, Uzbek 25%, Russian 4%, Other 6%**
Languages: **Tajik, Uzbek, Russian**
Religions: **Sunni and Shi'a Ismailite Muslim**

The Pamir mountain range towers over Dushanbe, the capital of Tajikistan.

Sept 1991 Independence from USSR

Nov 1991 Communist Party wins elections under Rakhmanov Nabiev; opposition excluded from power

Aug 1992 Demonstrators force Nabiev to resign

Sept 1992 Opposition coalition takes power; civil war breaks out

Nov 1992 Communist leader Imamali Rakhmanov wins disputed presidential election

Jun 1997 Peace agreement ends civil war; 60,000 were killed and 650,000 became refugees in Afghanistan and elsewhere

Nov 1998 Uzbek uprising; Tajik government blames Uzbekistan for supporting rebels

TAJIKISTAN

KYRGYZSTAN

The Kyrgyz people form barely half the national population of Kyrgyzstan. Like their Tajik neighbours, they have poor relations with the large Uzbek minority. But unlike Tajikistan, Kyrgyzstan has tried to keep the Russian population in the country, because it needs their skills to run the economy. Kyrgyzstan is unique in central Asia in that its post-independence leader, Askar Akayev, a physicist, was not a Communist Party politician. At first he followed a policy of economic and political reform, but ethnic tensions encouraged him to become increasingly dictatorial. Elections are rigged, opposition parties banned and their leaders are imprisoned. Many people accuse Akayev of fostering a personality cult.

JOINT ACTION

In 1999 members of the Islamic Movement of Uzbekistan (IMU) - a pro-Taliban fundamentalist group trying to establish an Islamic republic in the region - set up bases in Tajikistan and Kyrgyzstan. In response, the Uzbek air force bombed their bases in the so-called Battle of Batken. This increased tension between the three nations, until they signed a four-way agreement with Kazakhstan to fight terrorism and religious extremism. Both Kyrgyzstan and Tajikistan have allowed American military bases in their countries, as part of the international 'war against terrorism'.

FACT FILE: KYRGYZSTAN

Capital: Bishkek
Population: 5 million
People: Kyrgyz 59%, Russian 15%, Uzbek 14%, Tatar 1%, Ukrainian 1%, Other 10%
Languages: Kyrgyz, Russian, Uzbek
Religions: Sunni Muslim

Askar Akayev (1944–) became leader of Kyrgyzstan in 1990.

KYRGYZSTAN

June 1990 Major riots between Kyrgyz and Uzbek peoples

Oct 1990 Askar Akayev elected president

August 1991 Independence from USSR

Aug 1999 Battle of Batken: Uzbek air force bombs Islamic Movement Uzbekistan (IMU) bases in both Kyrgyzstan and Tajikistan

2000 Russian becomes an official language again to prevent Russians from emigrating

Feb–Mar 2000 Opposition parties banned during rigged elections

April 2000 Kyrgyzstan, Tajikistan, Uzbekistan and Kazakhstan sign agreement to combat terrorism and religious extremism

Aug 2000 Renewed fighting with IMU militants

Dec 2001 USA opens air base at Manas, near Bishkek, and another in Tajikistan, as part of its 'war against terrorism'

Uzbekistan and Kazakhstan are the two richest republics in central Asia, with the largest populations. Since independence, both republics have been run by former communists.

UZBEKISTAN

Uzbekistan is the most populated of the five republics. It has huge resources of gas, oil, coal, uranium and gold - the world's largest gold mine is at Murantau in the central Kyzylkum desert. It is also the world's fourth largest producer of cotton. Native Uzbeks form the majority of the population, but there are large groups of Russians, Tajiks, Kazakhs and others. Racial tensions have led to conflict as recently as 1990, but all such dissent is now strongly suppressed by the government.

FACT FILE: UZBEKISTAN

Capital: Tashkent
Population: 25.3 million
People: Uzbek 72%, Russian 8%, Tajik
 5%, Kazakh 4%, Other 11%
Languages: Uzbek, Russian, Tajik, Kazakh
Religion: Sunni Muslim

Islam Karimov, the former Communist Party boss, came to power in 1989. He was elected president after independence. The new constitution guaranteed human rights and freedom of religion, but both the nationalist Erk (Freedom) and religious Birlik (Unity)

Islam Karimov became president of Uzbekistan in 1991.

opposition parties were banned. Karimov now runs the country as a presidential dictatorship. His regime is brutal, and allegations of torture are common. His main opposition is the underground Islamic Movement of Uzbekistan (IMU), with close links to the Taliban. It aims to establish an Islamic republic in central Asia. The IMU is a serious threat to stability in the region.

1989 Islam Karimov becomes Communist Party boss

1989–90 Ethnic clashes in Fergana Valley

Aug 1991 Independence from USSR

Dec 1991 Karimov elected president

Dec 1992 Opposition parties and Islamic organisations banned

1996 Islamic Movement of Uzbekistan formed

Feb 1999 IMU bomb attacks in Tashkent

Apr 2000 Agreement to combat terrorism and extremism

Oct 2001 USA base at Khanabad to help fight the Taliban

Jan 2002 Term of president extended from five to seven years

Mar 2004 More than 40 killed in bomb attacks in Tashkent

UZBEKISTAN

ENVIRONMENTAL DAMAGE

The collective farms of the USSR have left an appalling environmental legacy in central Asia. In 1953 Soviet leader Khrushchev turned the virgin steppes of Kazakhstan into wheat fields. About 34 million hectares were planted, but the crops failed and the project ended. Even more damaging are the effects of irrigation in order to grow cotton in Uzbekistan and Turkmenistan. This caused soil salination (salt concentration), and polluted rivers with fertilizers and pesticides. One irrigation canal in Turkmenistan drained the Amu Darya River of one-third of its water, and the inland Aral Sea then shrank to less than half its size. The area is an ecological catastrophe.

The Aral Sea halved in size between 1974–97.

KAZAKHSTAN

Kazakhstan was the last former Soviet republic to declare its independence. Like many others it is a patchwork quilt of nationalities, many of whom were forcibly resettled in the republic from the Caucasus and elsewhere by Stalin. By 1959 ethnic Kazakhs were outnumbered by Russians, but since independence the immigrant Kazakhs from neighbouring states, and the departure of 1.5 million Russians, have redressed the balance. Today, Russians complain of discrimination as the government refuses to recognise Russian as an official language.

Kazakhstan has huge mineral resources, and is by far the wealthiest of the eight former Soviet republics discussed in this book. Like most of the others, it is ruled by its former Communist Party leader, Nursultan Nazarbayev. Changes to the constitution and electoral fraud have kept him in power since 1990. In 2000 the Majlis (parliament) even granted him special powers to advise future presidents when his term of office finishes in 2006, which will in effect ensure that he is president for life.

FACT FILE: KAZAKHSTAN
Capital: Astana
Population: 16.1 million
People: Kazakh 53%, Russian 30%, Ukrainian 4%, German 2%, Tatar 2%, Other 9%
Languages: Kazakh, Russian, Uighur, Korean, German
Religion: Sunni Muslim

KAZAKHSTAN

1989 Nursultan Nazarbayev leads Communist Party

Dec 1991 Kazakhstan independent; Nazarbayev is elected president

1995 Kazakhstan (with Ukraine and Belarus) gets rid of Soviet nuclear weapons left after break-up of USSR

Aug 1995 New constitution allows president to dissolve parliament and rule by decree; presidential term extended to 2000 without elections

Dec 1997 Capital moved, partly to control local Russian population

1999 Nazarbayev wins seven-year term in elections generally considered to have been rigged

TURKMENISTAN

Of the five central Asian republics, Turkmenistan is probably the strangest, for it is headed by one of the most bizarre leaders of any country in the world.

TRIBAL POLITICS

Turkmenistan is the southernmost of the Asian republics. In 1884 it was the last part of central Asia to fall under Russian rule. The Turkmen were largely nomadic and tribal peoples, and tribal loyalty remains strong today. The Tekke tribe live in the centre of the country, the Ersary live on the eastern border with Afghanistan, and the Yomud live in the west.

Conflicts between the tribes rather than with the two main minorities - Russians and Uzbeks - dominate social life in the country. But the imposition of Turkmen as the only official language, and restrictions on the right of Russian citizens to hold dual passports, have created recent tensions with the Russian community, and with Russia itself.

THE SUPREME LEADER

Turkmenistan is run by Saparmurad Niyazov, the former leader of the Communist Party, which is now called the Democratic Party of Turkmenistan. Niyazov has developed a huge personality cult (see box), censored the press and banned all opposition parties (even though the country is officially a multi-party democracy). In 1993 parliament voted to extend his term of office to 2002, a decision confirmed with a 99.99% vote in favour. Six years later, parliament removed a limit on his term of office: now he is president for life.

Although Niyazov might seem absurd, his rule is harsh. There are reports of the use of

TURKMENBASHI

Niyazov has styled himself *Turkmenbashi* ('father of all the Turkmen') and has encouraged an extreme personality cult. His portrait is on every building in the capital, on stamps and banknotes, on the first page of every book published and on every vodka bottle. He dominates all television broadcasts, his spiritual guide to living has been adopted as the national code and all university students must study his life and works. Towns, villages, canals, harbours and roads have been renamed in his honour, and his statue is everywhere. Most dramatically, he has erected a vast Arch of Neutrality topped by a 66-m column in the centre of Ashgabat. On top is a giant statue of him, made of pure gold. It revolves every 24 hours, ensuring that during the day his face always looks to the sun – or perhaps that the sun always follows him around!

Saparmurad Niyazov's presidential palace in the Turkmenistan capital, Ashgabat.

torture and mind-altering drugs, and all public and private meetings - even weddings and funerals - must be registered with the authorities. Any foreigner wanting to marry a Turkmen must pay $50,000, and no woman under 35 can emigrate unless she has had two children, so contributing to Turkmen ethnicity. At every festive occasion people have to chant a slogan that closely resembles the German motto used during the Nazi rule of Adolf Hitler.

RICH AND NEUTRAL

Turkmenistan was once the poorest of all the former Soviet republics, but it is now rich because of huge natural gas supplies and the export of cotton. Niyazov uses this wealth to keep himself in power, and to avoid foreign entanglements. He has declared the country neutral, and has had good relations with his neighbours (including the Taliban in Afghanistan). Since 2001 he has consistently refused to allow military bases or other support to the USA, in its 'war on terrorism' and against the Taliban.

FACT FILE: TURKMENISTAN

Capital: Ashgabat
Population: 4.8 million
People: Turkmen 75%, Russian 10%,
   Uzbek 9%, Kazakh 2% Other 4%
Languages: Turkmen, Uzbek, Russian
Religion: Sunni Muslim

TURKMENISTAN

1985 Niyazov first secretary of Communist Party

Oct 1990 Niyazov elected president

Oct 1991 Independence from USSR

June 1992 Niyazov re-elected president

Dec 1993 Parliament votes to extend Niyazov's term of office to 2002

Jan 1994 99.99% vote in favour

Dec 1995 UN recognises Turkmenistan's neutrality

Dec 1999 Niyazov made president for life

April 2003 Government removes right of Russians to hold dual citizenship and gives them two months to decide which passport to keep

April 2003 Restrictions on all private and public meetings

THE NEW GREAT GAME

One hundred years ago, the 'Great Game' was played out between Russia and Britain for control of central Asia. Today, a new 'great game' is underway: this time for oil and gas.

RESERVES OF WEALTH

Underneath and around the Caspian Sea lie the world's largest untapped reserves of oil and natural gas. Estimates range from 50 billion to 130 billion barrels of crude oil, and up to 460 trillion cubic feet of gas - 40% of the world's total gas reserves. New reserves are discovered all the time. Only Saudi Arabia, with 262 billion barrels, has more oil reserves than this.

The new 'great game' for oil and gas is being played out around the Caspian Sea.

International demand for these resources is huge. The existing supplies in the Middle East and elsewhere are being used up quickly, as demand soars in the USA, Europe and in rapidly industrialising states like India and China. This vast new source is particularly attractive to the USA, because most of the world's oil currently comes from the Middle East, which is politically unstable and often hostile to American interests.

THE NEW GAME

The four countries which share this massive wealth are Azerbaijan, Kazakhstan, Turkmenistan and Uzbekistan. But they also share a huge disadvantage: they are all landlocked. The nearest deep-sea port is almost 1,600 kilometres away, so lengthy pipelines have to be built. Pipelines bring vast amounts of money to countries they run through, not only in construction fees and increased local employment, but also in transit fees for each barrel of oil or cubic metre of gas that passes through. The best pipeline routes are north and west through Russia to the Black Sea, or south through Iran to the Persian Gulf.

When the four republics were part of the USSR all their pipelines ran through Russia, and Russia insists that any new pipelines must follow the same route. But the USA wants to strengthen these countries' independence from Russia, and keep any new oil and gas out of Russian control. It also refuses to support new pipelines through Iran, even though Iran already has a network of pipes from Turkmenistan

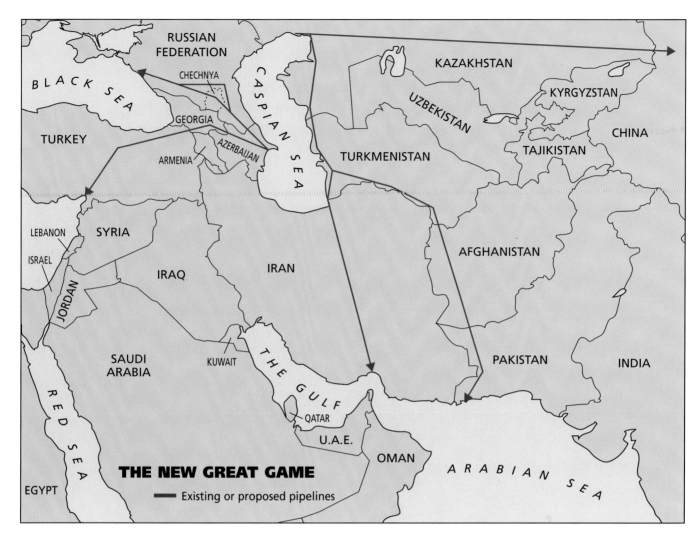

THE NEW GREAT GAME

— Existing or proposed pipelines

down to the Persian Gulf. Iran is seen as a deadly enemy of the USA - President George W. Bush has described it as part of the 'axis of evil' with Iraq and North Korea - so an Iranian route is politically impossible for the USA.

WHICH ROUTE?

In 1995 the US government supported a plan to build a gas pipeline from Turkmenistan through Taliban-controlled Afghanistan to the Pakistani coast. But the Northern Alliance - the main group then fighting the Taliban - refused to accept it. The plan was also opposed by Russia, which wanted Turkmenistan to continue using its pipelines. It was also opposed by India (which did not want Pakistan to extend its influence) and Iran (which wanted to export its own natural gas to Pakistan).

Since the Taliban fell in 2001, the plan has been revived. In fact, some commentators believe that one of the main reasons the USA invaded Afghanistan was to secure the country for its own economic interests, and so obtain easy access for American oil companies to the Caspian reserves. Another proposed route runs from Azerbaijan through Georgia and Turkey to the Mediterranean Sea, bypassing Russia. At present, pipelines run from the Caspian through Russia to the Black Sea and pass straight through Chechnya, which is why Russia is so keen to regain control of that area. China wants to construct a pipeline from Kazakhstan through to Shanghai.

With so much wealth at stake, as well as urgent energy needs, the new 'great game' has the potential to create massive world conflicts.

THE FUTURE

Since 1991, when the eight republics discussed in this book emerged into the post-independence world, huge changes have occurred in all of them. What will happen to them in the future? How will they survive?

Since independence, Muslims are now free to worship throughout the region.

LIFTING THE LID

The collapse of the USSR meant that the old quarrels and tensions repressed under Communist rule re-emerged. Disputes over boundaries led to war between Armenia and Azerbaijan; civil war wrecked Tajikistan; Chechnya and parts of Georgia fought for independence. Fundamentalist Islam - and Orthodox Christianity in Armenia and Georgia - replaced communism as the major belief, and ethnic tensions flared up in most countries.

Although communism disappeared, communist-style rule did not. Apart from Armenia, Georgia and Kyrgyzstan, all the states elected former communists to lead them after independence. The main political parties in Turkmenistan and Uzbekistan are communist parties with new names, while Tajikistan's ruling party did not even bother to rename itself after independence. Western-style democracy is weak, Turkmenistan and Uzbekistan are brutal dictatorships, and other states endure repression or lawlessness. Opposition mainly comes from terrorist groups trying to establish Islamic republics.

LANGUAGE

One consequence of the break with Russia has been the introduction (in many cases,

40

re-introduction) of Roman script. In Azerbaijan this is the fourth alphabet change in a century: Arabic was replaced by Roman, then Cyrillic, and then Roman again. Such changes cause problems with minority communities, and cultural and ethnic tensions are frequent in most states. They will cause more problems in the future.

NEW DIRECTIONS

When the eight were part of the USSR, policies were decided for them. Now Georgia looks west towards Europe, while the six Muslim nations look south (the five Sunni Muslim and Turkic states look to Turkey, while the Shi'a and Farsi-speaking Tajikistan looks to Iran). Only Armenia continues to look north to Russia.

THE BATTLE FOR OIL

The biggest change in the region is the influence of a new superpower - capitalist USA - to replace the USSR. The USA's 'war on terrorism' and opposition to fundamentalist Islam underpinned the invasion of Afghanistan. Its continuing military presence has a potentially explosive effect on central Asian politics.

The USA is desperate to control the massive oil and gas wealth of the region. So are many other nations. This will bring huge economic gains, but also causes problems. Will oil-rich Azerbaijan restart its war with impoverished Armenia? Will Russia succeed in subduing Chechnya? Water is an equally explosive issue. Together, oil, water and the clash of beliefs and political interests make this region a major flashpoint in the world - now, and for many years to come.

Oil brings huge wealth to the Caspian region, but also huge problems, too.

GLOSSARY

Abdicate To give up a throne, often voluntarily.

Autonomous Semi-independent part of a country, with some powers of self-government.

Caliphate Empire governed by one of Mohammad's successors (caliphs) as a ruler in the Islamic world.

Capitalism Economic system based on the private ownership of industry, finance and property.

CIS Commonwealth of Independent States, a loose association set up in 1991 to replace the USSR.

Collective farm Large farm owned by the communist state and managed by its workers, replacing privately owned small farms.

Communism Economic and social system in which everyone is equal, and where all property is owned collectively, by the people.

Constitution Written document setting out principles on which a country is founded and the rights its people enjoy.

Democracy Government by the people or their elected representatives, often forming opposing political parties.

Dictator Unelected head of state (or government) who rules by force.

Emirate Independent Muslim state, ruled by an emir.

Empire Group of peoples or countries governed by a single ruler or system.

Enclave Part of a country entirely surrounded by another country.

European Union Union of 25 European nations with common trade, currency and other links.

Federal System of government where power is shared between national and local or regional governments, which both have authority.

Fundamentalism, Islamic Movement that favours a strict interpretation of the *Qur'an* (Islamic holy book) and of *Shar'ia* (Islamic law).

Genocide Deliberate killing of one nationality or ethnic group by another.

Guerrilla war War conducted by an irregular, politically motivated, armed force.

Khanate Mongol empire, or a successor state, ruled by a khan.

Minority Group of people who form a distinct but small group within a nation and who are different from the majority of the population.

9/11 11 September 2001, the date when al-Qaida terrorists attacked the World Trade Center and two other targets in the USA. The USA then declared a 'war on terrorism' challenging Islamic fundamentalism and extremism around the world.

Nationalist Someone who is loyal or passionately devoted to their own country, and seeks its independence from foreign rule.

Nomads People who move with their animals in search of grazing land.

Personality cult Political movement or a set of beliefs based on the idolisation of a single leader, as with Stalin in the USSR.

Red Army The Soviet army.

Refugee Person who has fled from danger in one country to seek refuge in another, safer country.

Republic Country governed by an elected head of state called a president.

Show Trials Trials conducted on Stalin's orders in 1935–38 to liquidate his opponents and those he considered enemies of the state. About seven million people were arrested and tried on trumped-up charges, and about three million were executed, or died in labour camps in Siberia.

Silk Road Trade route stretching from eastern China to the Mediterranean Sea. Along the route were cities, towns and lodging houses where merchants could stay and conduct trade. Very few merchants travelled the entire length of the route, so goods changed hands many times before reaching their final destination.

Steppes Grassy plains of central Asia.

Superpower Country with overwhelming military and economic power, such as the USA or USSR.

Trade route Route along which merchants buy and sell goods.

Tsar Emperor of Russia.

USSR Union of the Soviet Socialist Republics, or Soviet Union, which existed from 1922 to 1991; commonly known as Russia.

INDEX